Shoes

Knowing Wh

MW01172057

by

Chester Williams, "The Airport Guru"

Table of Contents

Introduction

On an average day, I'd be providing airport etiquette classes in person because I help travelers lower their travel stress and anxiety level along with improving their overall understanding of what to expect when going through an airport. Out of nowhere, it seems like we are all living in a movie with the Coronavirus pandemic that we are all currently struggling with. On a good note, I've decided to spend my time in quarantine finally completing my first book for the traveling public. Since the cold reality is that most of us won't be flying for quite some time yet, you'll have plenty of time to read this book and learn a great deal about airline travel so you can be ready when we all finally get through this pandemic together.

Who is the "Airport Guru"?

I was born and raised in New Orleans, Louisiana. In August of 2005, Hurricane Katrina forced me to relocate to several different cities between Louisiana and Texas. Eventually, me and my family ended up in Texas in November 2005. I went to Conroe High my first three years of high school, but graduated from Spring High in 2009. Moving from my home in New Orleans was something to adjust to.

While in college, I fell in love with the study of psychology and sociology. I love the study of the mind and how others interact with individuals and in large crowds. It's amazing how body language can be a mouth full at times without even opening up one's mouth. While in school part-time, I found myself working as a floater for a company in Bush Intercontinental Airport in 2011. We had fast food restaurants, bars near departure gates and sit-down restaurants in almost all of the terminals. It allowed me to see and gain knowledge of the entire airport as I worked in different areas over the years. I learned a lot from others that worked for different airlines, the TSA and other companies as well.

Working in Bush Airport became an eye-opening experience for me. The atmosphere fell in perfectly with my interest and knowledge of psychology and sociology. Being around and helping different people of all ages, backgrounds and personalities all day was quite interesting. There wasn't a day that went by where I wasn't helping someone. Whether it was on my way to work while going through security or while I was working at my station.

It was never an issue assisting others, but I've noticed the average passenger I came across had the same, if not similar issues. Many had a tough, stressful time figuring out how or where to check-in and understanding how to process through the TSA security efficiently. There are also people who may not speak very good English or may be generally overwhelmed in airports. At first, I was slightly confused on how so many people struggle with getting through the airport. With all the information online and the many large airport signage, one would assume that most people would be more prepared and be able to understand everything. That's when I came up with the idea to create Guru Airport Services Airport Etiquette Class to teach people how to efficiently process through an airport as well as a concierge service to provide physical help in the airport as well.

Having a class allows people see live demonstrations of what to expect and gives them the opportunity to think a moment and ask questions. The airport is a fast paste environment and it makes people hesitant to ask questions. For the people that don't have time to attend in person and are always on the go, there is also a virtual class and more developing reading material as well.

As of now, although it is just me providing the concierge service, it gives others the chance to receive a physical extra helping hand in the airport to help with check-in. Traveling alone or by yourself with small children won't seem so scary. Losing a few hours of work just to help a family member at the airport for less than an hour will be a thing of the past. At least for people that fly or land in Houston, Tx.

Imagine people arriving at the airport more prepared. Think about less people holding up the lines while going through security. My mission is to not only cut the national wait-time in half, but to bring back the times where it was less stressful while in the airport. Even if it means traveling to speak in different cities, schools, business, or making material that is personalized to specific airports or specific travel leisure so one would know what to expect for each destination. I will do the best that I can in order to reach as many people as possible through different platforms in order to make sure passengers are informed and have a great experience while in the airport.

I'd like to quickly point out that the information provided here is focused solely on the Transportation Security Administration (TSA) based in the United States. Working in Houston, Tx at Bush Intercontinental Airport has allowed me to gain knowledge from TSA officers, airline employees, and other airport workers as well. Processing through security about six days a week for several times a day was an eye-opening experience for me, but soon this kind of work became second nature. This book is here to ease your mind, lower your airport anxiety, and potentially prevent any personal delays while going through airport security.

WARNING: Due to the adaptiveness of today's security protocols, the information provided in this book may be subject to change or may vary from airport to airport and/or personal experience.

How and Where to Enter Airport Security

The Transportation Security Administration, or TSA as it's commonly known as, has two types of security screening lanes: The Standard Lane, and TSA PreCheck Lane. Most people assume that there are several types of security screening lanes due to the several entry points based on a passenger's airline status and needs as well as seeing people on different tables around them. People can easily become confused by not paying attention to the airport signs describing which lane/entry point is which. Ask the nearest airline employee or TSA officer if needed. Also, when needing general information, not every airport employee will know why your flight was delayed or why TSA may have stopped you in the past. Some answers will have to be found from the source of your concern.

What does your boarding pass say?

In most cases, your boarding pass will tell you which entry point to use before you enter security and which lane you will use to be screened by security AFTER your boarding pass has been checked by TSA at the podiums. Most of the time, if your boarding pass doesn't indicate a specific status, then you will likely go down the standard entry point. As a reminder, no matter how many times you've exit the airport, you have to re-enter security and present your boarding pass and I.D. each time in order to come back in. You are able to leave out as many times as you want as long as your flight is still valid.

Having a certain airline status like First Class or Premier Access gives you a slight advantage of how quickly you get to the entry point of TSA Security. Once you reach the podium where they will check your boarding pass and ID, the ultimate decision of which TSA lane you are screened in depends on whether you have TSA PreCheck on your boarding pass or not (and if the TSA PreCheck Lane is even available or open).

The main objective is to figure out if you have a TSA PreCheck symbol or "TSA PreCheck" wording on your boarding pass and to find out where the entrance to the TSA PreCheck lane is. If you have TSA PreCheck along with an airline status, then make sure the airline status lane will lead you to the TSA PreCheck lane. In the coming sections, there will be different scenarios and security lane entry points based on a given status in order to gain access through TSA Security.

NOTE: If you are PreCheck and find yourself in the standard lane as TSA is checking your boarding pass, then ask the TSA officer if there is a PreCheck Lane available and where it is. If there is no TSA PreCheck lane available and you are processing through the standard lane screening, TSA may ask you to show your boarding pass to the officer at the X-ray table to possibly receive some Expedited Screening. Expect to possibly remove electronics from your carry-on and receive standard screening since you are in the standard lane, as the TSA can have some fairly unpredictable screening measures at times.

Entry Points Based Off Boarding Pass Status or Specific Status

- Normal or Basic Economy Board Pass (no status)
- Gate Pass (no status) – Used mainly to gain access through security to assist escorting a family member or minor to or from the gate.
- TSA PreCheck (status)
- Clear (status)
- First Class (status)
- Business Class (status)
- Active Duty Military - Some airports have active duty military go through shorter entry points if you are in full uniform and present your military I.D. Always ask if there is a military entry point available. Never assume there is one, as all airports are different.
- United Airlines Status - Global Services, Premier Access, Premier 1K, and more
- American Airlines Status - Concierge Key elite AAdvantage, Platinum AAdvantage, Executive Platinum AAdvantage, Oneworld Emerald and more
- Emirates Airline Status – Skywards Silver, Gold, and Platinum and more
- Wheelchair Access (specific status)
  - Passengers in a wheelchair, walker, etc.
- Airport Employees (specific status)

NOTE: DO NOT abuse status entry points based on your or other people's status by trying to bring 5, 6, or 10 people from your travel group with you unless the specific airline or airport allows it. Some, if not all others may possibly get turned around, especially during major holiday seasons. Most exceptions are parents with kids, people with senior citizens, or a small adult ratio of 1:3 or 2:5 (the ratio tactic still varies depending on airport). All other scenarios are reviewed on a case-by-case basis depending on the airline or airport. Some airports have people directing traffic to make sure people are in the correct lane. The best option is to simply ask first instead of getting turned around at the last minute after already waiting in line.

Scenario - Your ticket says Premier Access and TSA PreCheck. Which lane do you choose? Premier Access or TSA PreCheck?

Answer - It depends on how the line (aka, zigzag maze of ropes) is set up. If both lanes lead to PreCheck, then choose the quickest lane since you have options. When you reach the TSA podium, they will divert you to TSA PreCheck after checking your boarding pass and I.D. If Premier Access doesn't lead to PreCheck, then head straight for the PreCheck entry instead. Most airports have the PreCheck lane moving pretty quickly anyways so using the PreCheck entry lane may be the best decision most of the time.

Scenario - There is a family of five with two adults and three children, who are 14, 17, and 18. Four of the family members are TSA PreCheck, but the youngest child is not. Can they stay together and use the PreCheck entry point and go through the PreCheck lane since they are a family, or do they have to separate?

Answer - Only TSA PreCheck passengers with a boarding pass that scans PreCheck can go through the PreCheck lane. Although, a passenger who is <u>12 years of age or younger</u> is allowed to process through PreCheck with a parent or guardian who is PreCheck even if the child doesn't have PreCheck on their boarding pass. Whether the family decides to partially separate or not, the 14-year-old has to enter through the standard lane nonetheless. Most of the time, I see one parent or older sibling enter through the standard lane with the non-PreCheck family member. Also, if the parent feels that the child is responsible, they can allow them to go through the standard lane alone. Depending on the airport setup, you may be able to see one another enter through security from a distance and also wait for your counterpart in the back if you go through security before the other person.

Scenario - A passenger claims they are always TSA PreCheck, but for this particular flight they are not. They proceed down the TSA PreCheck entry point to try and gain access to the PreCheck lane. Once they get to the podium, they try to show their Global Entry card to proceed forward, but are quickly denied and forced to use the standard lane. Why were they denied access to PreCheck and what could they have done better?

Answer - Only passengers with a boarding pass that says and scans PreCheck (or children 12 and under with a PreCheck guardian) can enter through TSA PreCheck. The passenger should have entered the standard lane instead. Having a Global Entry card doesn't mean you automatically gain access through PreCheck. The TSA acknowledges the Global Entry card only as a form of identification. Only when going through U.S. Customs do you show a Global Entry card to access a faster lane. The passenger should have used their TSA PreCheck number (located on the back of their Global Entry Card) at the kiosk to potentially print a new ticket that says PreCheck. Even though having a Global Entry card means you paid for PreCheck, you have to enter your KTN (Known Traveler Number) number during booking or in this case, at the kiosk. 95% of the time, the first new printed boarding pass will register PreCheck. If it doesn't register on the first attempt, then try two more times. If it still doesn't work on the third try, then just go through the standard lane. Sometimes it just doesn't register.

Scenario - Over the last several flights, a passenger brings the same set of toiletries in your carry-on bag. This particular time, TSA stops their bag and explains that they have discovered that one of their LGAs (Liquid, Gel, Aerosol, Cream, Paste) is 4oz and is oversized and not allowed as a carry-on item. They inform them that regardless of last time, the rules are still the same and that 3.4oz or 100ml is the max for the item. Should the passenger be allowed to keep it since they have traveled with it before?

Answer - Rules are rules. The best analogy I can explain is like driving on the highway. Almost everybody speeds at some point on the highway, but not everyone gets caught while speeding. When speeding and finally caught, not everyone gets a ticket. Some cops give people a warning and others give tickets. When someone gets pulled over, no one says, "The last cop let me go." Most of the time, they accept the fact that they've done something wrong and they accept the consequences. When getting stopped by the

TSA after having discovered a prohibited item, ask what options you have and accept the consequences of your actions.

Providing Valid Documentation to TSA

Passengers who are 17 years old and younger do NOT need to show I.D. to the TSA unless they appear to look 18 years old or older as some teens may appear. If you or your child looks 18 but doesn't have a valid I.D. then have a birth certificate or other valid document that proves the child is under 18 years old. When providing an I.D. the TSA only needs ONE valid acceptable I.D., and here are some examples below.

- Passport or Passport Card
- Driver's License/State I.D. - Make sure your driver's license or state identification is Real I.D. compliant by 10/1/2021. Visit tsa.gov/real-id for more information or if the deadline changes due to the Coronavirus.
- TWIC Card, Military I.D., Global Entry Card, Permanent Resident Card, and more

If you don't have a valid form of I.D., then arrive an hour or so earlier than normal and have at least three of these items with your name, current address, and other personal information to confirm your identity. Try to make sure it's the physical document. Pictures of documents typically aren't accepted. Below are some documents you can bring to help verify your identity.

- Birth certificate
- 1 up to date credit or debit card
- Social Security card
- Health Insurance card
- Bill with name and address

- Voter Registration card
- Prescription with your name
- Sam's or Costco Card (face)
- Old, expired I.D. (face)

Having three of these items (Try to have at least one face I.D.) will help you get through security if you've lost, forgotten, or just don't have any acceptable form of I.D. When renewing your driver's license, TSA accepts expired driver's licenses for up to one year after expiration. If you provide the temporary paper driver's license, you'll get held up because it's not an official acceptable form of I.D for the TSA. Still bring it if that's all you have. It's better to bring additional forms from the list above to help you get through quicker. As stated on the Tsa.gov website, there is a possibility you may not be able to enter security in the event that the TSA cannot verify your identification during the verification process.

Getting your Boarding Pass and I.D. Checked

Showing your document to the TSA can be an easy process or it can be a difficult one. As long as you prepare yourself properly, you'll be fine. When you are at the front of the line, PAY ATTENTION. If multiple officers are checking boarding passes, then you should be looking from left to right for someone in either direction to call you forward. The key thing is making eye contact and/or listening for someone possibly yelling "Next!"

Make sure you have your boarding pass and I.D. in hand BEFORE they call you up. Have your I.D. out of your wallet with your boarding pass. Being ready at their podium speeds things up a bit as opposed to flipping through your wallet or purse to find your I.D. With the entire world being on edge about germs, I would hope that people refrain from putting their I.D. or boarding pass in their mouth right before they hand it off to the TSA as I've seen it happen a great deal while heading to work.

In most cases, TSA only needs your current airport departure boarding pass. Try to refrain from handing the officer a stack of boarding passes all at once or handing them a boarding pass folded where they have to unfold it several times just to see it. It's quicker and more efficient when the officer receives one boarding pass and I.D. at a time and in most cases, one person at a time. A great technique if you are with a family or a large group is to approach in pairs.

If you are in a group, make sure everyone in your group holds their own boarding pass and identification. Even if you are typically the responsible one holding on to everyone's boarding pass and I.D.; everyone who is at least about six or seven years of age and older should be able to hold their own boarding pass at the last minute for a few moments unless they are incapable of doing so. Try to pass them out while you are in line BEFORE the TSA calls you forward. Unless you are a family with infants/toddlers or with someone who has medical needs, in most cases, it's best to approach their podium individually or in pairs. Depending on the officer, in some cases, they may allow more than one person at a time as long as it doesn't become too crowded for them. If you have a group of more than 3-4 people, ask the officer if they would like the group or for everyone to come one at a time or in pairs. Remember, they can technically check only one person at a time.

After your boarding pass and identification is handed back to you, place both the I.D. and boarding pass in your carry-on unless directed to keep in hand. Putting your boarding pass away is nothing new. Most people assume they need it out, which is why you may see 99% of people holding both their I.D. and boarding pass in their hand. A great deal of people tends to lose their I.D. in between the entry point of security and right after they pass through security. If you lose your boarding pass before or after it is checked by security, then you can typically reprint a new boarding pass at the check-in counter or at your gate without a problem. A select few airlines may charge a small fee for a new printed boarding pass at the gate. You can also use your phone and have a mobile boarding pass as backup if you lose your paper boarding pass.

TSA Standard Lane Screening

You can have all the airline status in the world, but if you don't have TSA PreCheck, then you'll likely be in the standard lane taking off your shoes, jacket, and emptying your pockets. If you do indeed have TSA PreCheck on your boarding pass and you decide you want to stay with your travel companion or group in the standard lane, TSA may ask you to show your boarding pass a second time to the officer at the table. Expect to have standard screening. Airports vary, but being PreCheck in a standard lane, the only perk is possibly being partially expedited. Since you're in the Standard Lane, you have to remove whatever they ask from your luggage into the bins.

Average travelers dread this lane because of all the things it requires them to do. Not to mention, this lane is typically slower than being in the TSA PreCheck as well. While witnessing firsthand what slows people down inside security, I would hope you would use these techniques to help you get through quicker and more efficiently. After you've received your boarding pass and I.D. from the TSA, start putting all your personal, loose, and miscellaneous items that are typically in your pants' and shirt pocket inside your carry-on. No, this is not a new rule. Many people are accustomed to using the bins at the last minute that they are unaware that they are allowed to use their bag for phones, keys, wallet, coins, belt, and whatever else you have on you that you need to remove from your person. Also, if you have a big enough jacket with zippers to close the pockets, you can put your things inside your jacket as well. Think of your jacket as another bag. You want to be more secure and be able to grab all your items in one or two strokes on the other side.

It's not about getting dressed and putting things where they originally were while on the conveyor belt. It's about having everything securely packed and being able to grab everything easily while walking to the benches in the back to redress. Using the bins for everything you own slows down everything. Just imagine those times when you are finally through security and you are ready to grab your belongings to catch your flight but the person in front of you is taking their sweet time getting dressed, blocking you from grabbing your stuff because the belt is full. Then the TSA can't move anything out of the machine because everyone is on the belt at the same time.

If you are even able to place your jacket and shoes in your bag, you can do that as well. It's no different than the clothes and other things that are already inside your bag. While going through security, your property can typically become lost or forgotten and even sometimes stolen. Now, I know you may have a system because you fly every week, but I've seen and heard a lot of things happening to passengers that are unfortunate and it can happen to anyone. I've heard stories from passengers where they end up calling the airport or TSA lost and found or the police to file a report for someone out of state for a stolen item. Remember, I've spent 8+ hours in an airport for 5-6 days a week for over 6 years. The average person probably spends less than 20 minutes going through security and less than 2-3hrs in the airport overall. Use this knowledge to your advantage to become more at ease and prepared when in an airport.

Standard Lane Rules

Here are the main things you will do in the standard lane. If possible, do most of what you can BEFORE you get to the table. Preparation is key. The slowest passengers are the passengers who wait until the last minute at the table before getting situated.

1. **Empty pockets** - As described earlier, try to do this before you reach the table. By "Empty all pockets" they mean ALL items, including non-metallic items as well. Loose cash can be placed in your bag or held in your hand. If you are holding something in your hand, be prepared to show the officer. Sometimes they may ask you to put your wallet in a bowl through the machine instead of allowing you to keep it in your hand. Putting it deep in your carry-on may be your best bet.

2. **Remove open sweaters and jackets** – Outer wear typically comes off and pullovers that are light jackets and hoodies are typically fine.

3. **Remove all footwear** - Bring travel socks since you have to remove your shoes. Those who are 12 years of age or younger as well as 75 years of age and older are allowed to keep their shoes on unless they trigger an alarm on a machine. Depending on the airport, showing your TSA PreCheck boarding pass in this lane MAY allow you to keep your shoes on as well.

4. **Remove belt** - This is recommended but not always required. I would always remove it unless you

have a high success rate with it. All belts are different. You can also ask the officer what they suggest since they see belts all day. A simple belt can be the cause of whether or not you get taken aside by security or not. Imagine having to walk back and forward through the metal detector multiple times or get patted down because of it. I say remove unless the officer says otherwise.

5. Jewelry - It stays on unless someone tells you specifically to remove it. If you do have to remove it, place it in your carry-on so you won't lose it. The scanner is mostly fine with jewelry, but most bangles are the worst on metal detectors. Remember, not all metal is bad.

6. Remove electronics - Take out electronic devices larger than a cell phone. Cell phones are a visual aid to take out larger electronics and can typically stay inside your bag unless directed otherwise. Place devices flat and either side by side in the bin or individually in separate bins. Don't stack the devices and don't place anything above or below them either. If you are unsure of certain electronics, just ask. Below are some examples:

> Kindles, e-readers, tablets (A tablet is a screen without a keyboard that has computer capability), Laptops, Bluetooth speakers, Nintendo Switches, CPAP Machines

7. Remove toiletries - These are your bathroom products, but anything that is liquid, gel, aerosol, cream, or paste-like qualifies as a part of your toiletry bag as well. Make sure they are all 3-1-1 compliant (3.4oz or 100ml or less). Solid toiletry items like stick

deodorant don't apply to the 3-1-1 rule since it's a hard item. In some cases, they may not ask you to remove them if they are travel-size. In most cases, anything over 3.4oz must be in your check-in luggage. In the event you have an oversized toiletry item, inform the officer at the table before pushing your property inside.

8. Food - If you're wondering, the answer is yes, food is allowed, but expect it to be inspected by security from time to time. Solid foods and powder substances are fine of any size. Be cautious of certain types of slushy, liquid, pasty food over 3.4oz because they are not allowed in your carry-on (Read note (b) below if liquid, pasty, slushy food is over 3.4oz). If you have a large amount of food, sometimes it's better if you show it in the bin or put your food in one bag opposed to two or more bags. When you have it in multiple carry-on bags, then you may possibly have multiple bags pulled aside. When it is visible in a bin, it is sometimes less likely to get pulled aside if the TSA can already see it outside your bag. This can make things quicker as opposed to waiting for an officer to look inside your bag(s).

    a. Baby water, juice, food, formula, and breast milk are allowed in your carry-on at any size. Try to bring a reasonable amount just for the flight. There is no real limit for breast milk, but expect it to be pulled for an additional check.

    b. Note - You are allowed to bring FROZEN water as long as it's FROZEN when it goes through the machine. This technique can be applied to anything slushy, liquid, and pasty, which have to be below 3.4oz and in your toiletry bag. With it being a solid(frozen), it does not have a size limit nor does it have to be in your toiletry bag. No, this is not a new rule. It's been on the TSA website for quite a while. Feel free to browse the prohibited and non-prohibited items list sometime. If you are unable to freeze your items or keep them frozen long enough to pass through security, then you can place it in your check-in luggage or leave it at home. If it becomes a liquid before passing through, then it becomes a prohibited item. The officer will ultimately make a judgment call on whether or not there is too much liquid.

9. **Double check yourself and your bag** - Check if you have water or any other prohibited items or weapons in your carry-on bag or pockets. Make sure your gun is either at home or in your car and not in your carry-on. A friend of mine told me he forgot his gun in his carry-on once while going through PreCheck. He not only lost his flight, but also lost his PreCheck status and received a fine in the mail. He was too embarrassed to tell me the amount, but from his bad attitude, I knew it was in the thousands. Looking further into it, you can be fined up to $13,669 per violation per person.

10. **Strollers and car seats** - The child must come out of the stroller or car seat. Make sure you remove any loose items in or under the car seat or stroller. Most infant car seats and some collapsible

strollers fit inside the X-ray. Some strollers have removable wheels to help make them fit as well. If it doesn't fit or you are unable to lift it while traveling alone with your child, then ask for assistance with lifting it on the table or you may have to move it aside and wait to have an officer physically inspect it.

11. **Wheelchair passengers** - Inform the officer at the table if you or the person you are with is able to stand and walk unassisted. If you are unable to walk, inform the officer at the table. Expect to wait for an officer to escort the person in the wheelchair to the other side of security to provide a pat-down. Even while in a wheelchair, you still need to empty your pockets and remove your shoes. If you can walk, then an officer will physically check your wheelchair and pass it to you on the other side. If you have a wooden cane, then an officer will most likely allow you to use it while processing though security. If possible, allow the TSA to put your cane through the x-ray first so they won't have to do it later on the back end of you going through security.

12. **Passengers with pets** - If you have a pet inside a carrier, then you will have to remove them from the carrier and place the carrier inside the X-ray machine. Try to place the carrier ahead of all your other things so you can put your pet away first on the other side. Both the person and the pet will walk through the metal detector. You can either hold your pet and walk through or walk them on a leash. Be cautious that some leashes and harnesses may trigger the metal detector. If you are unable to handle your pet out of the carrier or without a leash or

harness, then inform the officer at the table and they will inform you of your other options. While getting dressed on the other side of security, never place or leave your pet inside the carrier while it's on the moving conveyor belt.

13. **Place belongings inside the machine** - Place all closed bags directly onto the table unless directed by the officer to place all bags and items inside the bins as some airports do require all bags to go inside bins. If you have a tote bag that doesn't close all the way, then try traveling with a small jacket to help close it better, use a bin or simply travel with a bag that can close all the way to prevent things from falling out. I've seen phones, money, IDs, credit cards, and lots of other things fall on the ground from people not securing their bag or improperly putting things inside the bins.

14. **Double check pockets again** - completely empty.

15. **Stay with your belongings** - Unless directed by an officer to walk away, continue to stay and push your belongings at the table until they are inside the machine unless you are traveling with the person behind you who can assist guiding your belongings inside.

16. **Scanner screening** - Almost everyone will be using the AIT (Advanced Imaging Technology a.k.a. The Scanner). Those who are 12 years of age and under will typically go through the metal detector with their parents. 75 years of age and older typically use the metal detector as long as they don't have any

metallic implants or medical devices that won't allow them to. Make sure to inform the officers at the table of metal implants or devices so they can direct you to the proper screening machine. If you choose to not use any machine or you are simply unable to use a machine or complete a certain task, then inform the officer at the table. You can also ask for further details about the scanner, metal detector, as well as further information on what to expect when getting a full pat-down. Below is what to expect after using the scanner and metal detector.

- When the scanner shows a Green Screen with "OK" on the scanner's monitor it means you're good to go unless you have items in your hand to inspect. Look at the screen when stepping out of the machine and wait for it to change or wait for the officer to clear you to leave.

- When you alarm the scanner, the monitor will show a white avatar(body) with Yellow Boxes which means an officer of the same gender will check and pat down those highlighted areas. The officer sometimes has to cover a sensitive area which includes the groin, buttocks, breast, and inner thigh as well. Make sure to inform the officer of any medical devices or painful areas before being patted down.

- All you have to do with the metal detector is walk through it like a doorway without bumping the sides or making it sound off and you are clear to go. Don't stop in the middle of the machine. Just walk through it at a normal pace. The machine not sounding is the "ok" to keep going. If it does sound, stop immediately and listen for instructions.

17. Cleared from screening - After you are cleared from using the scanner or metal detector, proceed to gather your property from the conveyor belt. If you are able to, then consolidate items to lesser bins and take the bin and get dressed in the back on the benches. If you are quickly getting dressed on the belt, try to place empty bins in the cart at the end of the conveyor belt or in a return slot if available. Getting dressed slowly or leaving empty bins on the conveyor belt can hold up other passengers from receiving their property if there is no room to push out other items.

18. Luggage or bin missing - Here are some reasons why you may be missing a bag or bin:

1. It may have been possibly pulled aside by TSA for additional screening. If your bag is pulled for additional screening, gather everything else and wait at the

back table until called upon. Rushing the officers because your flight is boarding will not make them move faster. TSA is far more concerned with safety, so have patience.

2. It may have been sent through the machine a second time.

3. You may have left it on the table and not pushed it entirely though.

4. Someone may have mistakenly taken it. 95% of the time, it's probably an accident if it was taken by someone else. There is a small chance that you will be next to someone with a similar bag or laptop as you. When you notice this, try to create space, place the item or bag in between your other items, or let someone else go ahead of you. If you are still unable to locate your bag on the other side, politely ask an officer for assistance. Remembering what lane you came through and what time it was when you first pushed your property through helps the TSA search quicker on the camera as well. I lost my airport badge once after going through security and they were able to find it by looking at the time I came through.

These steps are the general guidelines of what to do in the standard lane of the TSA. Things are subject to change and may vary depending on airports. Remember, different houses, different rules. Different days, different rules. Security was never meant to be consistent. We all don't have the same house key, nor do we all have the same passcodes. My grandmother told me to remove my shoes before I came to her living room, but my grandfather didn't mind when my grandmother wasn't around. Don't expect security to be the same every time you fly. Researching your airport and airline as well as Tsa.gov website to help with future travel.

Every time you process through any security, remember these words. "The less you have out, the less you have to worry about. Out of sight, out of mind. The less you have out, the quicker you'll be and the less likely you'll lose or forget something"

Entering TSA PreCheck

This is by far the easiest of the two when going through the TSA security. For clarification, having TSA PreCheck does NOT exempt you from any type of screening. It just means you are in an expedited process and typically may not have to do as much as you would as if you were processing through the standard lane. Everyone still has to follow the 3-1-1 rule as well as the prohibited item list. At the end of the day, everyone has to get screened accordingly. I thought employees were treated differently, but boy was I wrong.

Most people in this lane have either paid to be in this lane, have received PreCheck randomly based on flight status, have possibly received PreCheck based on someone else's itinerary, or sometimes they are just an employee going to work like I was. As a passenger, no matter how you got it, whether you paid for it or not, you will not receive PreCheck 100% of the time. There are random times where you can get kicked out of PreCheck and it won't register on your boarding pass due to the randomization of the system or certain itinerary changes or possible last-minute changes before your flight. Now if you've paid for it, then you have an opportunity to possibly regain your PreCheck status, as stated earlier. If you realize it's not on your boarding pass before you arrive at the airport, then you can use your airline app or website to plug in your KTN (Known Traveler Number) or you can use the kiosk at the airport and manually print a new boarding pass. This works 95% of the time.

Note: TSA uses unpredictable security measures, both seen and unseen, throughout the airport. All travelers will be screened, and no individual is guaranteed expedited screening. This means that there is a small percentage that you won't be PreCheck and you may even go through a random screening while going through security.

TSA PreCheck Boarding Pass Tips

Everything moves quickly in the TSA PreCheck lane. When I'm heading to work, the five seconds people take to remove their I.D. and boarding pass from their pocket at the last minute can seem like five minutes sometimes. Make sure you're not holding up the airport flow and have your boarding pass and I.D. are ready when you get to the front. Remember, 17 years of age and under does NOT need identification for TSA purposes (If you look 18 then have some type of valid documentation on hand just in case) and 12 years of age and under can use the PreCheck lane with a TSA PreCheck guardian.

If you're using a mobile boarding pass, try to wait until you arrive at the airport to pull out your board pass. I believe there has been an update on some airline apps that mess with the barcodes if you have the app open for too long and sometimes it won't scan correctly or register your PreCheck status in their system. To regain a fresh barcode, close the app completely and reopen it. If it is still unsuccessful, then the officer will ask you to go to the kiosk and manually print a boarding pass. Also, if you have a cracked screen, the boarding pass may not scan if the crack is running through the barcode. A friend of mine learned this the hard way and almost missed their flight. Have a printed boarding pass from home or from the kiosk just in case.

If you are using a print-from-home or an airport-printed boarding pass, make sure the barcode isn't smudged, faded, or ripped. The TSA may not be able to process it if it doesn't scan. This happens when your printer at home or the airport kiosk is running out of ink. The kiosk running out of ink doesn't happen too often, but this is something to be aware of. As stated earlier, don't forget to safely put your I.D. and boarding pass away after you've been checked.

TSA PreCheck Lane Rules

1. Metal detector screening - Everyone is typically going to use the metal detector unless told to use the full body scanner. Inform the officer at the table, before you use any machine, if you have any metal implants, medical devices, or anything that may not allow you to use either the metal detector or the scanner.

2. Place large metallic items inside carry-on - Since you are passing through a metal detector, you will have to remove large metallic items from your person. Sometimes, there are bins in PreCheck you can use, but most of the time, it's just small dog bowls. You can either use a dirty airport bowl or your carry-on bag. Try to use your bag as much as you can and a bowl as a last resort. As stated earlier, "Less you have out, the quicker you'll be." As quickly as the lines move, you don't want to be that passenger holding up the line trying to fill a bin or dog bowl with random things from your pocket. I would rather lose something in my bag than in an airport. If you trigger the metal detector, step back out and wait for instructions from the officer on what to remove or what to do. Most of the time they know what's going on. Below are common things to keep an eye out for:

    a. Common items to remove from pockets: phones, keys, cans, headphones, and sometimes coins if you have too many. As a former server, I always had way too many coins in my pocket.

b. Items that MAY or MAY NOT ring - Belts, certain large-face wristwatches (small watches are typically fine), certain wallets with metal or embedded RFID blockers and bangle-like bracelets or large hoop earrings.

3. Everything stays inside of your luggage - No need to remove electronics or toiletries. In certain cases, if you have an item that you continuously get stopped for, then you may want to explain to the officer at the x-ray table that you have an item that may you pulled aside. They may say leave it in anyways to keep the flow going and may inform the next officer ahead of time on the matter. Try to give yourself a little extra time if you know your bag will be searched. Some common items that may require additional screening are baby formula/water, protein powder, and frozen items.

a. In the event that the TSA pulls your bag to remove things like a laptop, your bag may be too cluttered for them to see its contents. Especially if you typically travel with you entire office in your carry-on luggage.

4. Keep your shoes on unless they trigger the machine's alarm - Be aware that all shoes won't make it passed the metal detector. Always try your shoes so you know what passes versus what shoes you may have to remove for the

next time. If you make it 2 out of 3 times with one pair of shoes, then don't expect to make it every time. Bring travel socks just in case you have to remove your shoes. Below are different types of footwear to consider when traveling.

- Most tennis shoes are fine.
- Shoes with large amounts of metal may not pass the metal detector half the time. Men and women's dress shoes, boots, some heels, steel toe shoes/boots, kids' skate tennis shoes, as well as other types may have metal shanks in the sole of the shoe.

5. Belts stay on - Be aware that not all belts pass through the metal detector.

6. Light jackets and suit jackets stay on - Most light jackets, hats, scarves, and cardigans are fine unless it's too bulky for the officer you are approaching. The officer will inform you if you need to remove something that qualifies as bulky. Each judgment varies. Clothing comes into question around the winter time or if you are traveling somewhere cold. If you use the scanner in this lane, I would remove the outermost clothing to minimize your chance of a pat-down. I learned the hard way when I asked to keep my light jacket on while in the scanner. My jacket alarmed the scanner below my belt and the officer had to pat me down near my groin area. Ultimately, it made me late and it could have been avoided if I took their suggestion to remove it before being scanned.

7. **Double check yourself and your bag** - One would say that holding up the line for a bottle of water in your bag on the PreCheck lane would deem you as a rookie passenger. There is nothing wrong with double checking yourself one more time for a cell phone in your pocket or a water in your bag.

8. **Luggage or bin is missing** – Remember not to panic. As stated earlier, check with an officer on if your property was sent through the x-ray again or pulled aside before you assume that it is lost or stolen.

Some airports may not have a PreCheck lane at all or they may be closed. If you are unable to tell whether or not you're in a PreCheck lane, ask the officer at the table. When coming from an international flight, some checkpoints may not have PreCheck or honor TSA PreCheck boarding passes to keep on your shoes if you are in a standard lane. After leaving customs, ask someone at the check-in counter or a TSA officer if a PreCheck lane is available.

These steps are a general guideline of what to do in the PreCheck lane for TSA. Things are subject to change and may vary depending on what airport you're in. Remember different houses, different rules. Different days, different rules. Security was never meant to be consistent. We all don't have the same house key, nor do we all have the same passwords. There was a time my grandmother would always say remove my shoes before I came to her living room. One time (noticed I said one time), my grandfather didn't mind. Don't expect security to be the same every time you fly. Research your airport and airline as well as www.tsa.gov to help with future travel.

Every time you go through any security checkpoint, remember these words: "The less you have out, the less you have to worry about. Out of sight, out of mind. The less you have out, the quicker you'll be and the less likely you'll lose or forget something."

Quick Airport Tips

1. **Dress comfortably** - Shiny, flashy clothes, hard-to-remove shoes, and jewelry may not work in your favor when going through security. Everyone is welcome to dress how they please, but be ready to take certain things off.

2. **Invest in travel programs** - Having Global Entry and Clear is a great combination on top of also having an airline status as well.

3. **Stop following people** - When going through security, look for open lines and not just the closest person you see. You may end up in a longer line when following behind others. Treat the security lanes like the highway. Look left and right for an open lane to pass other passengers.

4. **Invest in cases for your laptops and tablets** - Get cases for your electronics in order to minimize your items directly touching the dirty airport bins where people typically place their shoes as well as prevent scratching and other damage. When using a case, only the device can be in the case and

no other items, such as paper, chargers, and books. Be mindful that some officers may still ask you to remove it from the case.

5. **Use a small zip lock bag or pouch for your small items** - Use a small bag for your phone, keys, wallet, and coins and then place them in your carry-on luggage. You'll may find that it is quicker to gain access to it opposed to having a scavenger hunt inside you bag.

6. **Bring travel-size hand sanitizer or some disinfectant wipes** - With the Coronavirus affecting our everyday lives, you can never be too cautious. Until further notice, the TSA has allowed <u>(1) passenger each (1) bottle of hand sanitizer to not exceed 12oz. in your carry-on luggage</u>. Expect it to be pulled for an additional check since it's considered over-sized.

7. **Bring a sweater** - Airports can be pretty chilly especially near the gates.

8. **Clear out your travel bag before your next flight** - You don't want to travel with extra or unwanted items in your bag.

9. **Buy a luggage scale** - It's a good habit to weigh your luggage before you arrive at the airport. You don't want to be on the floor at the check-in counter trying to switch things into different bags just to avoid the 50lbs+ baggage fee. Be smart, plan ahead.

10. **Don't over pack** - Imagine your zipper on your luggage breaking or trying to move things from your

carry-on to your check-in bag. Don't be *that* passenger.

11. ## Evaluate the cost/time of a prohibited item - When getting stopped by the TSA for having an oversized toiletry or other prohibited item, is the item worth the cost and time it takes to leave out of security to pay the extra checked baggage fee (unless you have a free checked bag) just to keep the item and go back through security again?

12. ## TSA discard options - When something is not allowed through security, you have several options on how to proceed:

   a. ## Check it - Leave security to put it in a checked bag. You would typically forfeit one of your current carry-on bags to check in the item at the ticket counter. Remember, make sure the item is worth it to pay to keep it and that you still have time before your flight departs.

   b. ## Take it to your car

   c. ## Give it to a family member or friend - If you have a family member or friend outside of security, then the TSA can hand the item in question to that individual. TSA typically does not hold items for long, so the person receiving the item should be available on the spot. You can also leave security yourself and wait for the individual to arrive.

d. **Mail it to yourself** - Not all items qualify to be mailed. Ask the officer if it is possible for your case. Average items mailed items are pocket knives.

e. **Discard it** - Your last option is to surrender the item to the TSA and allow them to discard it. Most of the time, you are unable to retrieve the item once you have surrendered it.

13. **Pack Quick Meds and a Small First Aid Kit** - Allergy meds, Pepto Bismol, and other over-the-counter meds can come in handy while in the airport, so be sure to bring some with as shopping at the airport can be pricey.

14. **BE ON TIME!!!** - Being on time means being inside the airport 2-3 hours before boarding (2 hours for domestic and 3 hours for international). This is the recommended time which allows you to handle personal delays that may occur. Returning to your car to retrieve a wallet would become possible if you show up early. During major holidays and major city events, it would be 3-4 hours. If you fly often enough and know your airport well enough, then you may be able to shave off 30 minutes.

15. **Research your airport** - Researching your airport will save you time and help prevent you from getting lost. Most airports have a layout of the terminals, gates, restaurants, and retail stores online or on Google Maps and possibly other mobile maps as well.

16. **Download your airline's app** - Downloading the app for your airline will allow you to receive alerts about your flight and to learn more information about your flight.

17. **Be more patient in an airport** - The most patient people are the ones who are on time. Don't become impatient and blame the long airport lines because YOU are running late or because YOU are having a bad day. Expect the unexpected and take everything one step at a time.

18. **Every airline has a boarding start and end time** - There is typically a 15 to 30-minute gap from the start of boarding to before the doors close or before you lose your seat. Just because your flight is boarding in 20 minutes doesn't mean you are necessarily going to miss your flight. Unless you hear your name over the airport speaker, then you are most likely fine.

19. **If you need to run, THEN RUN!** - Don't be shy and worried about what others will think when they see you running. You can either try to be cool but maybe miss your flight, or you can become a track star in the airport and make your flight! If you're in a group, try to allow someone to go ahead to see if they will wait for the rest of your party. It's not guaranteed, but it's worth a shot. Just be mindful of the others around you when you're sprinting to the gate.

20. **Be polite to others** - Nobody likes a rude or disruptive passenger. Whether it's a gate agent,

restaurant server, officer, or another passenger, you never know who you may need help from while in the airport or on the airplane. It costs absolutely nothing to be kind!

21. **Enjoy your trip!** - Never let anyone or anything ruin your day. Whether you are traveling for work, family, or pleasure, try to make traveling a fun experience. I promise that you'll experience something hilarious or interesting during your travels. No matter what happens throughout the day, the day is what you make it, not how you take it. You control your happiness. Not the events or people around you.

Conclusion

It is my sincere hope the insights presented in this book has allowed you to become more prepared, aware, and mindful when in an airport and going through TSA security. If you're interested in learning more about what I do and would like to support my mission in providing more content and services in order to cut the national wait time in half for both lanes and create a better experience for all air travelers, then follow my website and social media accounts listed below. Don't forget to leave a review and please be sure to share and encourage others to check out my book in order to give them the opportunity to become more prepared for their next flight!

http://www.guruairportservices.com

Facebook - https://www.facebook.com/GuruAirportServices/

Twitter - https://twitter.com/GAServiceLLC

Instagram - https://www.instagram.com/guruairportservices/

Sincerely, The Airport Guru

Made in the USA
Columbia, SC
06 January 2022